6 Ste
Blood
Cholesterol

...and make your heart smile

First Edition 251020

Instagram: *@not_spam_fritters*

Tel/text: 07725 121 121

MIX
Paper from responsible sources
FSC® C018072
www.fsc.org

About the Author

Brian M Stratton has been writing reference and text books since 1988. He is a Freeman of the City of London and a member of their Guild [no jokes about funny handshakes, please].

Born in 19 hundred and typing error, he moved to 'that there London' in 1976. He managed to embed himself into the community and, so far, he's blended in successfully without revealing his northern heritage. His wife says: 'What about the NUFC tattoo and the coals in the bath?' Ha! That's not true! It's not coal. It is seasoned artisanal logs from sustainable forests, actually. So as my Geordie Grandma would no doubt say: "Hadawaynshiteman!"

Combining northern grit and London savvy, he is now a well balanced individual – he has a chip on each shoulder [joke].

Previously, his only exercise was jumping to conclusions, but Brian now enjoys keeping fit and healthy by regular exercise, walking, researching and exploring historical London. And sometimes writing about himself in the third person.

Here's what people say about this book:

"...I like how it's not overly serious and is simple to understand..."
Priyesh, 32, Pharmacist, London

"...Encouraging, informative, inspiring and clever... I love the personal touches... and it's as if someone is chatting with you..."
Janet, 52, Iowa, USA

"...No huge paragraphs, so it doesn't feel like you're wading through loads of information..."
Cal, 48, Oldbury

See back cover for further reviews

Also by the Same Author

Latest Publication: *12 Bridges.London*

A book of self-guided walks from twelve of the capital's iconic bridges. For more details about publications, and to order, please contact: Brian M Stratton: 07725 121 121
Instagram: *@12bridges.london*

Acknowledgements

Endless thanks go to my wife Mrs S for her patience and for having the fortitude to read through the numerous drafts of this book. She never tired of hearing those three little words: "Read this, love."

And of course, the focus groups and proofreaders – especially LB – who had to trawl through my drivel and make some sense of it.

Much as a Formula 1 car has a team of mechanics, this old banger is very grateful to all the health professionals who keep him ticking over: Andrew [optician], Andy [dentist], Chris [physio], Sue [podiatrist] and GPs Dr Sen and Dr Lizzie.

Contents

Introduction 7
What is Blood Pressure? 9
What is Cholesterol? 12

Step 1: Measure 15
Step 2: Manage 23
Step 3: Monitor 29
Step 4: Diet 33
Step 5: Exercise 49
Step 6: Lifestyle 55

Alcohol 61
Smoking 63
FAQs 65
Q&A with the Author 69
Glossary – Explanation of Terms 75
Summary 78
To Do List 79
And Finally... 80

...High blood pressure – hypertension as doctors call it – rarely has noticeable symptoms. An estimated 5 million people in the UK are living with undiagnosed high blood pressure...

Introduction

The inspiration for this book has come from the fact that I discovered I had high blood pressure and cholesterol – the impact it then had on my life – and the changes I made, and continue to make.

This book explains how you can lower your blood pressure and cholesterol which will then significantly reduce the possibility of stroke or heart attack.

Stroke and heart attacks are often known as the silent killers due to not having any warning signs.

I've therefore come up with some ideas and changes that you can choose to use, or not. I've also provided reasons that I think make sense and are logical.

I've had more than my fair share of health scares over the years. Two life-changing and potentially fatal events were ones over which I had no control whatsoever.

By comparison, issues of high blood pressure and cholesterol [life-threatening matters] are something that I [and you] can control and prevent escalating into a fatal event.

If you are aware of health issues you can then manage them and – to use a shocking cliché [I try and avoid them like the plague] – you should 'own' them.

High blood pressure – hypertension as doctors call it – rarely has noticeable symptoms. An estimated 5 million people in the UK are living with undiagnosed high blood pressure.
Source: bhf.org.uk British Heart Foundation

But if untreated, it increases your risk of serious problems such as heart attacks and stroke.

In the UK, someone suffers a stroke every 5 minutes. Most are survivable but many people are left with life-changing disabilities and/or health issues, meaning they have to rely on partners and carers to continue functioning.

So prevention is absolutely better than cure. Men are more likely to be affected – more die because of stroke than through testicular or prostate cancer.

Naturally, before changing any aspect of your health regime always consult your GP first and follow their professional advice.

What is Blood Pressure?

Blood pressure is the force at which blood is pumped around your body.

This is happening all of the time as your heart beats. As the blood flows, it puts pressure on the blood vessels which carry the blood away from the heart.

Blood pressure is measured as the heart pumps and then as the heart relaxes.

Blood is pumped from the heart and circulated through the arteries – think of them as tubes – to deliver oxygen and nutrients throughout the body.

The blood is then circulated through veins back to the heart, keeping it alive and functioning by supplying it with oxygen and nutrients.

The coronary arteries can become blocked – high levels of cholesterol can do this – and this restricts the blood flow.

This in turn makes the heart work even harder to force the blood through narrower tubes.

Blockages in the arteries – just as if they were furred up pipes – can reduce or stop the flow of blood and oxygen to the heart and brain. And without treatment the heart muscle begins to die, and the brain ceases to function.

When blood pressure becomes dangerously high, it can cause a TIA [Transient Ischaemic Attack – a mini-stroke], stroke or heart attack.

It's like the boiler in your house – see it as the heart – if radiators come to be blocked – this causes extra pressure on the boiler which could cause a complete breakdown. You might get some warning signs – the boiler runs slowly or makes a noise which in turn alerts you that something is wrong and you can take action.

The worst that's going to happen if you don't take action is that you'll get cold and then have a large bill to fix the boiler. Then you whinge a lot and move on with your life.

Similarly in a car, if the engine is struggling there will be red lights which come on to warn of danger.

If no action is taken, extra pressure on the engine could cause a catastrophic breakdown.

The worst that's going to happen is you get stranded by the side of the road and get a large bill to fix the car. Then you whinge a lot and move on with your life.

On the outside of a human body there are no warning lights or other signs that there is high blood pressure.

The worst that's going to happen is that you could have a heart attack or stroke and suffer a fatal breakdown.

You then don't move on with your life.

End of.

Blood pressure therefore needs to be monitored on a regular basis, managed and controlled as necessary.

This will give you the best possible chance of minimising the possibility of stroke or a heart attack.

Don't let your blood pressure control you.

You can control it.

Control the controllables.

What is Cholesterol?

It's a golden-yellow substance, which has the texture of fat and would feel smooth and slippery between your fingers.

It is made in the liver. And can also be found in some foods.

Too much of it can block the arteries – think of these as clogged up pipes – and this can lead to a stroke or heart attack. Not enough blood gets to the heart, starving it of oxygen.

There are two types of cholesterol:

- **HDL** – High Density Lipoprotein [good – helps clear the cholesterol out of your system]
- **LDL** – Low Density Lipoprotein [bad – clogs up your arteries with cholesterol]

The body needs both types to function.

If there is too much LDL – the bad stuff – circulating in the blood this can cause disease of the arteries which in turn can increase the risk of developing CVD [Cardio Vascular Disease] such as coronary heart disease, angina, stroke and heart attacks.

Having high levels of LDL cholesterol is just one of a range of factors that increase risk of cardio vascular disease.

Other factors include: being overweight, drinking excess alcohol, smoking and lack of exercise, all of which will affect cholesterol, as will high blood pressure.

Statins [tablets which help to reduce cholesterol and are the most common medication for this condition] will reduce the risk of CVD but cannot eliminate it altogether.

It's a combination of factors.

Lifestyle changes need to be brought into the equation as well.

Making just one change won't necessarily make any difference, but making all possible changes can make some difference.

It's an holistic approach – where all of the elements [diet, exercise, stress management and so on] contribute to the whole positive life-enhancing effect.

1

> ***...The benefit of taking your blood pressure regularly is that you'll be aware much earlier of any changes. You can then take any action necessary to resolve issues...***

Step 1
Measure

The starting point is to measure your blood pressure and cholesterol.

Blood Pressure | Measuring

This will then give you the starting point. Is it normal, too high or too low?

For blood pressure:

Normal: Range 120/80 – 139/89mmHg
Too High: 140/90mmHg or above
Too Low: 80/60mmHg or below

The first figure [140 for example] is the Systolic and the second number [90 for example] is the Diastolic.

Systolic pressure is when the heart is pushing the blood around the body.

It's the contraction of the heart muscle.

Systolic comes from the Greek 'Systole' meaning contraction or drawing together.

Diastolic is the resting pressure between heart beats.
The relaxation of the heart muscle. Diastolic comes from the Greek 'Diastole' meaning drawing apart.

Blood pressure is measured in units of millimetres of mercury and expressed as, for example: 140/90 mmHg [Hg is the symbol for mercury].

Doctors would refer to the above reading as '140 over 90'.

This relates to the time when the measuring device was a glass tube filled with mercury and the blood pressure would push the mercury up the tube and this was measured against markings on the tube [think about a temperature gauge, which operates on a similar principle].

Blood pressure tends to rise as we age, so a reading of 140/90 might be reasonable for someone aged 60, but not for a 40-year-old.

Having measured your blood pressure, you can then decide on the best course of action and formulate a plan as to what, ideally, it should be in order to minimise risk and maximise health.

You can measure your blood pressure in a variety of ways:

- At home with a portable monitor
- At the doctor's surgery
- At a pharmacy
- At a hospital

Be aware that 'white coat syndrome' may give you a false reading.

This can occur when you're not in familiar surroundings.

White coat syndrome [*see Glossary*] is when you are anxious and nervous because of the situation – doctors used to wear white coats, hence the name. The reading taken whilst in this state might be unnaturally high and not a true reflection of what your blood pressure actually is.

Taking your blood pressure at home should reflect your normal blood pressure.

Taking it with a portable monitor is the preferred option as you will feel more comfortable when at home and in familiar surroundings where you can create a quiet environment.

Before taking a reading, you may find the following guidelines helpful:

- Seated and quiet with both feet on the floor is the best way to get a true reading.
- No talking or interaction with others and minimise your screen time.
- Each time, rest for 3 minutes before taking a reading.

Discard the first reading – see it as a 'throat clearer' in much the same way as a barista would reject the first coffee of the day or a barman would 'clear the pipes' before serving the first beer of the day.

Take readings at the same time each day – generally in the morning, and use the same arm each time for consistency.

Be systematic and consistent.

Take three readings and either average them out or note down the lowest one.

See over page to note your blood pressure

Record your blood pressure here:

1

2

3

Perhaps put a chart on the fridge – you can plot points and see how the graph is going – as a line – and look at the trend rather than just individual numbers.

Is there an upward trend, downward trend or are the readings staying consistent?

Additionally, you could note them down in a diary or on your phone, in the 'Notes' app for example.

The benefit of taking your blood pressure regularly is that you'll be aware much earlier of any changes. You can then take any action necessary to resolve any issues

Cholesterol | Measuring

This can be measured at home with self-test kits, at the doctor's surgery or at a pharmacy.

The self-test kits require you to prick a finger and place a drop of blood on a strip of card and then assess its colour against example colours to ascertain your 'number'.

They are 'once-only' use and not as accurate as having the test done at the doctor's surgery or at a pharmacy.

When you have the test done at the doctor's surgery, it will be a fasting [where you don't eat for at least eight hours before], or non-fasting test, depending on what the doctor has advised.

The blood test could also highlight other health issues e.g., liver and kidney health.

You'll usually have to wait a few days to get the results, which the doctor will go through with you.

The overall result, and then whether that's good or bad, is a calculation following the measurement of the two types of cholesterol.

Calculating the ratio between Total Cholesterol [TC] and HDL is an easy way to get an idea of whether your cholesterol levels are healthy.

For example, these are my figures from a recent test:

TC Total Cholesterol: 3.85 mmol/L [healthy is below 5 mmol/L]

HDL Cholesterol: 0.99 mmol/L [healthy is above 1.0 mmol/L]

Divide the TC number by HDL to provide your cholesterol ratio: [3.85 ÷ 0.99] = 3.8 mmol/L

TC/HDL ratio: 3.8 mmol/L [healthy is below 4, and above 6 mmol/L is considered high risk]
Source: [heartuk.org.uk]

The mmol/L figure refers to millimoles per litre of blood. A millimole is a thousandth [thath eathy for you to thay] of a mole which is a basic unit of measurement.

Everyday's a school day!

Incidentally, don't make the same mistake as I did when phoning a pharmacy.

I'd been researching an aspect of London's history when cholera [entirely different from cholesterol] was prevalent, so I had that on my mind when phoning. I asked if they did cholera tests and heard the girl say to one of her colleagues: "There's a guy wants to know if we do cholera tests, what shall I tell him?"

A senior pharmacist then came on the line, obviously worried, and said: "I understand you wanted a cholera test?"

By this time I'd realised my mistake and quickly reassured him that it was in fact a cholesterol test that I wanted.

Record your cholesterol here:

1

2

3

TIP

This is the starting point. Your journey begins here. What you do from this point on could save your life.

REFLECTION

It might be possible – in discussion with your doctor – to first of all try lifestyle changes and manage without drugs.

To see a difference, try non-medical methods for three months and monitor to see how much difference they make.

2

...Using drugs to prevent heart and circulatory disease is not a substitute for maintaining a healthy lifestyle...

Step 2
Manage

Once you know what your blood pressure and cholesterol numbers are, you then have to decide what action needs to be taken to manage them.

If your **blood pressure** is found to be higher than the normal parameters of 140/90 it can be managed by prescribed medication and advice regarding diet and lifestyle.

If your **cholesterol** is higher than the normal parameters of 3–6 it can also be managed by prescribed medication and advice regarding diet and lifestyle.

The medicine prescribed for lowering cholesterol is a group of drugs called statins.

Over 8 million people take statins in the UK and it is the most commonly prescribed drug in the UK.

Statins can help to lower the LDL [low-density lipoprotein] or 'bad' cholesterol in the blood.

This can reduce the risk of CVD [cardiovascular disease], which is the leading cause of death and disability in the 40–70 age group in the UK.

The higher the adherence to statins, the lower the mortality rate. In other words, once prescribed, keep taking the tablets.

Statins work by reducing the liver's production of cholesterol.

There is always the possibility that statins could result in an increase in weight – maybe doubling the chances of putting on weight.

How so?

People can sometimes see statins as a 'free pass' whereby if taken, and cholesterol improves, the other aspects of health management can be ignored. So you go back to eating the fatty foods, drinking, taking no exercise and so on, expecting your LDL cholesterol to stay low. But this isn't the case.

Rather than a 'free pass' [a licence to eat whatever you like and take no exercise], it could turn out to be a 'hospital pass'.

Using drugs to prevent heart and circulatory disease is not a substitute for maintaining a healthy lifestyle.

Keeping fit and healthy helps the medicines to work more effectively.

It's a combination of actions which will help you maintain a healthy lifestyle *[see Step 4]*.

Even if your BP is lower than the recommended maximum of 140/90, it's worth monitoring on a regular basis to see if there are any changes.

If so, you can then take the necessary action to stabilise it.

Please note that the blood pressure and cholesterol tablets can have side effects, as follows:

Statins | for Lowering Cholesterol

Fluvostatin and Simvastatin are two of the most commonly prescribed statins.

Commonly reported side effects include: difficulty sleeping, headache, stomach discomfort or joint/muscle pain.

Discuss any side effects with your GP or pharmacist.

Avoid eating grapefruit and/or drinking grapefruit juice when taking statins *[see below for reasons]*

Blood Pressure | Tablets

Amlodipine is one of the most commonly prescribed tablets.

Commonly reported side effects include: fluid retention, swollen ankles, headache, tiredness, muscle cramps.

Amlodipine – avoid eating grapefruit and/or drinking grapefruit juice.

The reason is that grapefruit reacts with the medication and reduces the body's ability to break it down, meaning that higher levels of Amlodipine can increase the side effects.

This reaction is specific to grapefruit and doesn't apply to other citrus fruits, such as oranges, lemons or limes.

Views and Observations

"...I was expecting and had read about swollen ankles but still a bit annoying when it happened... I followed advice and cut the tablets in half and this helped... another side effect was unexpected but equally welcome and put a spring in my step if you get my drift... I now call them my blood pleasure tablets... It's made me quite a hit with the older ladies, or vintage bintage, as I jokingly call them... I've certainly set hearts – and bingo wings – aflutter!"
Eddie, 63, managed BP and Chol

"...Once I realised I could fine-tune the dosage by cutting pills in half I was able to control the ankle swelling..."
Jenny, 53, managed BP and Chol

"...I've been on the tablets for about twelve years now... some side effects such as mild fatigue, muscle ache and lack of libido... difficult to know though whether it's the tablets or just age?!"
Michael, 60, managed BP and Chol

TIP

Once medication has been prescribed to manage your blood pressure or cholesterol ensure you continue to take it at the correct time and the correct dosage each day. This will maintain its effectiveness. Continue to make changes in other aspects of your lifestyle as well: exercise, a balanced diet, reducing alcohol intake and so on.

It's an holistic approach – all aspects combining together, rather than one element.

"…Please note that the blood pressure and cholesterol tablets can have side effects…"

3

…Monitor for any changes and if there are significant changes consult your GP…

Step 3
Monitor

Having taken your blood pressure – and managed or stabilised it – you then need to monitor it on a regular basis.

This could be every day, week or month so that there is a consistency to the monitoring.

Blood pressure readings can vary considerably throughout the day or evening depending on your activities and level of stress.

Having measured and managed your blood pressure, by monitoring it on a regular basis you can assess any patterns or 'spikes' that can alert you to changes to your heart health that need to be assessed.

Don't be too alarmed if there are slight changes [+ or – 10%] on a one-off basis.

If there are high readings [+20%] on say, three consecutive days, that would be the point at which to contact your GP for a check up to see if there are any underlying issues as to why the higher readings have occurred.

Reflect on your life-style over the past week and try to recollect if there have been changes to diet, any stress-causing incidents and so on.

Cholesterol can be monitored on a three/six monthly or annual basis.

Keep a record of it – either in your diary or on the 'Notes' app on your phone.

Monitor for any changes and if there are significant changes consult your GP.

TIP

Set aside a time to take your blood pressure regularly and consistently. Perhaps fit it into your morning regime: shower, shave [gents only?], sit and take your blood pressure.

Diarise your cholesterol readings and plan for three, six or twelve monthly checks.

"...Don't be too alarmed if there are slight changes on a one-off basis..."

4

...The best food is that which has had the least intervention from farm to table...

Step 4
Diet

Assess your diet and see what realistic changes need to be made to help reduce blood pressure and cholesterol.

Phase 1

Keep a food diary and list everything you eat and drink.

Be honest with yourself when you do this and write down what you eat and drink during a week.

And yes, that does include the hobnobs with your coffees, the cheeky pint at lunchtime and the Friday cakes in the office.

When you see your food consumption written down it can be quite astonishing. You'll say things like: "Did I really eat all that?" Yes, you really did.

As for me, I was brought up on man food. A full English was the 'ambrosia of the gods'.

A bacon sandwich, made with thick white doorsteps, real butter and brown sauce was the ultimate fast food. Add in fish and chips, curries, a Big Mac and a cheeky Nando's and you've got a recipe for... for what? Disaster, stroke or heart attack. Yes, it is food porn. An instant quick fix, then looking for the next hit. The difference is that with this type of food the money shot could be your final hurrah.

When I was growing up in the 1960s, fine food was a prawn cocktail starter, steak and chips as a main and to follow, black-forest gateau. Yum. And at home it could be spam fritters and Smash followed by Angel Delight [butterscotch flavour, of course].

Bear in mind that in the 1950s [my early years] it was still within ten years of the end of World War 2 so there was an air of austerity and food was still not in plentiful supply.

You ate what was put in front of you. There was no choice. It was take it or leave it. And woe betide you if you left it. You'd likely as not get a back-hander. And that was just from your Mam.

There was no time for faddy eaters or special diets.

And as for vegetarians in the 1960s, they would be mocked and laughed at, and offered a huge range of options on the menu: 'Nah! Just an omelette.'

Fast forward to today's world of vegans, vegetarians, pescatarians and flexitarians. Not forgetting pedestrians of course... what do they eat? Walkers crisps no doubt...

I wonder what my Geordie Grandma – think Jimmy Nail in a floral housecoat, but with more attitude – would make of today's healthy food.

A favourite saying of hers was: "Hadawaynshiteman!", which translated for the benefits of southerners, means something along the following lines: 'I'm not sure I fully believe what you're telling me...' or: 'Jog on'.

Every Sunday afternoon we'd visit for tea which generally was spam fritters.

I can't remember what accompanied this but I'm pretty sure it wasn't a peppery rocket salad with pea-shoots or kale.

Probably baked beans.

And what would Grandma make of the current trend for healthy eating and super foods?

Firstly, I'd explain to her what each of the types of healthy eaters are.

Vegans: eat only non-dairy products, no meat and no fish or eggs or all other animal-derived ingredients.

This diet is considered to be higher in fibre and lower in cholesterol than an omnivorous diet

Vegetarians: eat vegetables and fruit but not meat, fish or poultry

Pescatarians: eat fish and dairy but not meat

Flexitarians: eat mostly fruit and vegetables but occasionally meat

Omnivarians: eat everything – meat, fish, etc

And then I'd explain to Grandma what the healthy 'superfoods' are now.

Grandma: "Superfoods you say? Howay man, is it not just over-priced shite made trendy by Shoreditch tw*ts in east London? The same ones that have twirly moustaches, trousers that are too short for them, no f*cking socks, and those wanky sit-up-and-beg bikes?? And menus priced up without the £ sign, such as: '.6' for oat milk. Are they not just pretentious and greedy f*ckers???"

To be fair, Grandma might have a point there. She always was very astute and ahead of her time, and didn't suffer fools [gladly or otherwise].

So, in the interest of balance, I've done some exhaustive in-depth research [OK, a quick look on Google]. Here you go:

Superfoods are so-called because they are good for digestion being high in fibre and nutrients and low in starch.

They are plant-based, have low glycemic levels which also provide a slow release of glucose/energy which keep you fuller for longer and prevents 'sugar crashes' which can lead to snacking/bingeing between meals.

They also help to maintain your immune system and keep you regular.

The Romans had a saying: *"Et Saturamati bene cacas"* which as every scholar knows [I didn't] means: "Eat well and shit well" and is obviously a good saying to live your life by.

So here's a list of superfoods which will help you to do just that.

Phase 2

Study the food list below and see what you can incorporate in order to eat a more healthy balanced diet.

Couscous is... so good they named it twice. It's a grain: a tiny pasta made of wheat or barley.

Usually cooked by pouring boiling hot water onto the couscous which increases its size to rice-like grains.

Couscous is very similar to semolina, which many of us remember as a school pudding. Also there was tapioca, which we called 'tadpoles' due to the lumps which looked like frog spawn.

Couscous is usually served as a base or accompaniment to vegetables.

Kale is... a member of the cabbage family. Curly kale is the most popular.

Usually cooked by frying for 2 mins, baking in the oven until crisp, or steamed in a colander over boiling water for 4 mins.

Kale is usually served as an accompaniment to things such as couscous. It can also be used as a salad component in sandwiches.

Quinoa is... an edible seed that has become increasingly popular among health conscious individuals.

It is pronounced 'keen-whaa' rather than 'quinn-oh-a' because when you find out how much it costs you say: "'Kin Wha'? How much??"

Usually cooked by bringing to the boil in water, and then simmering for 10 minutes so that it absorbs water and swells to twice the volume.

Quinoa is usually served as an addition to things such as couscous and salads.

Spelt is... a type of grain which the Romans called 'the marching grain' due its high energy content.

Usually cooked by bringing to the boil and simmering for 30 minutes, so that it is tender but still has a 'bite'.

Spelt is usually served as a rice or risotto-like base or accompaniment to vegetables.

Chia seeds are... tiny black seeds from the plant Salvia Hispanica. The Aztecs and Mayans in South America prized them for their ability to provide sustainable energy.

Usually cooked by bringing to the boil and simmering for 3 minutes, or sprinkled raw on salads or included in smoothies.

Fact: Chia seeds can absorb up to 27 times their weight in water.

Chia seeds can be sprinkled on salads and breakfast cereal or incorporated into smoothies.

Falafel is... ground chickpeas which are formed into spheres [about the size of golf balls], and mixed with various spices.

It originated in the Middle East and has spread world wide.

You could make them from scratch but it's far easier to buy them and just heat them up, or even eat cold in a salad.

Falafels are usually served with salad, or maybe even in a flatbread or wrap.

Hummus is... a dip or spread made from cooked and mashed chickpeas blended with tahini, lemon juice and garlic.

Again, you could make it from scratch but far easier to buy it ready-made.

Hummus is usually served as an accompaniment to a salad, as a dip to be used with crudités – batons of raw vegetables such as carrots and courgettes.

Hispi is… a type of green cabbage which has a softer texture and sweeter taste than standard cabbage. Currently very fashionable and seen on all the best menus.

Hispi is usually served as an accompaniment to things such as couscous or rice or potatoes.

Note: Superfood supplements are available as powders, tablets and liquids. Probably better than not taking them, but fresh superfoods would always be best.

Grandma would probably say: "And people pay good money for these things do they? And can you get them in Fine Fare?"

"For tea tonight I thought we'd have spam fritters and beans. None of your fancy London ways here. So is that OK for you?"

Family in unison: "Aye, champion!"

And as a hot drink later on we'd have Camp coffee [a brand name, not a flamboyant hot drink], which grandma kept on a shelf in the pantry. This bottled coffee was in a liquid form and was a type of ersatz coffee with supposedly a walnut taste. Tasted like dishwater with a faint residue of… something indefinable and musty.

If we were having tea to drink, it would be dispensed loose from a futuristic/rocketshaped container attached to the wall. Pressing an oblong-shaped button would allow a spoonful of tea leaves to drop into the pot.

Vimto, Sarsparilla, Dandelion and Burdock [WTF is that anyway?] and Tizer were the soft drinks of choice, often delivered by the pop man who would do the rounds of residential streets in a lorry or van.

After recent events though, getting something off the Corona man now has a distinctly more sinister meaning...

Salt

Salt is a killer in food, and reduction in your salt intake will reduce risk overall.

The reason is that salt causes the body to retain fluid – blood is 92% water and 8% blood plasma proteins – and the extra volume causes the heart to work even harder.

This is made worse by clogged arteries – the tubes carrying the blood – and the narrowing and hardening of them through age and other factors.

You'll often see salt and sodium listed on food packaging.

Are they both the same or is there a difference?

While the words "salt" and "sodium" are often used interchangeably, they are not the same.

Sodium is a substance that affects blood pressure and is the main ingredient in salt. Ordinary table salt is only 40 percent sodium. The other 60 percent is another mineral, chloride.

It is the sodium part of salt that is necessary to maintain water balance in body tissues.

However, too much sodium can increase fluid retention and elevate blood pressure.

Sugar

Too much sugar in your diet can lead to – amongst other issues – an increased risk of heart disease, diabetes and fatty liver.

Weight gain is a key factor, so consider reducing your sugar intake: drink water rather than fizzy drinks – energy drinks etc, eat whole fruits rather than smoothies, eat plain yoghurt rather than flavoured ones, choose nuts and fruits rather than sweets. Eat cereals with reduced or zero sugar content.

Preparing healthy meals at home with fresh ingredients can help you cut back on sugar.

Talking of which, most of what I ate when I was growing up was mainly processed and high in fat and salt.

Examples being: sausage and beans, spam, gristly [and grisly] chops, fatty stews, Smash ready mixed mashed potatoes. Any vegetables used were boiled to within an inch of their lives, with all nutrients long gone. Imagine the lovely smell of boiled cabbage [~~ear~~ noseworm]. Fine dining it wasn't.

Phase 3

Processed foods should be avoided wherever possible.

When food is processed it usually involves changes to the nutritional composition through being preserved or fortified in some way.

On the one hand, it does give foodstuffs a longer shelf-life but it robs them of their freshness, vitality and nutrient content.

Unhealthy levels of sugar, salt, sodium and fat are added to help preserve them and make them taste better.

Too much can then lead to obesity, high blood pressure, raised levels of cholesterol, diabetes and other complications.

Best to avoid them altogether. Examples include: sausages, bacon, ham, sausage rolls, cakes and cookies, frozen pizza, sugary cereals, all of which are processed food.

Examples of healthy non-processed foods are: avocado, walnuts, beetroot, kale, spinach, fruits and berries, kiwi fruit, chick peas, nuts and seeds, broccoli, cucumber, cauliflower, tomatoes, oily fish such as tuna, salmon, sardines and mackerel.

All of the above, particularly kale [and optimism] were in short supply in the north east in the 1960s.

And we were so poor we thought cutlery was jewellery.

It was eating as fuel without any thought as to its calorific or health values.

These days, there is such a variety of choice that it's so much easier to eat well and healthily.

And yet people don't – we tend to get stuck in behavioural grooves. We stick to what we know and like.

Ideally, we should have gone from Smash potato [processed mashed potato] to smashed avocado [completely unprocessed].

The best food is that which has had the least intervention from farm to table.

Note: Maintaining a healthy weight will also help reduce your blood pressure and cholesterol levels.

Being overweight affects your blood pressure because the heart has to work harder to keep the body going with heavier weights.

Imagine walking upstairs and carrying two bags of sugar, then doubling and doubling that. It puts more and more strain on your heart.

We eat with our eyes and so you can exchange one unhealthy food for a healthy one that looks like it.

For example:

Chips – Polenta chips – you can buy a block of polenta for 75p and cut it into chips which can then be baked in the oven. They look and taste like ordinary chips but are a healthier alternative.

Or sweet potato fries are another alternative to regular chips.

Milk – try lower fat alternatives such as soya, almond, oat, coconut and so on.

Use the milk both in tea or coffee and on your cereal.

Cereal – try muesli or porridge [which are low in fat and salt] rather than processed cereals which are often high in sugar and fat.

Cream – try fromage frais.

Ice cream – try frozen yoghurt instead.

Crisps – try crackers with zero salt or fat.

Biscuits – have a banana instead.

These are just a few ideas – maybe try a 'thought shower' and brainstorm with others to come up with alternatives.

Naturally, you wouldn't want a completely joyless eating experience so maybe 'treat' yourself once a fortnight with a takeaway or one of your favourite food treats.

Another way is to view pub/restaurant menus online so that you can visualise or picture the dish before you go. If not, the temptation is that once you get into the pub or restaurant you might be seduced by the smell of grilled meat or barbecued dishes, and then your instincts kick in and you're persuaded.

By making the decision before you go out – away from the aromas and atmosphere of the pub or restaurant – you've already set your mind on your healthy choice of food.

One way to help lower your cholesterol is to consider the Benecol range [spreads, yoghurt and yoghurt drinks].

Their site states: Benecol is the only range of foods to contain 'plant stanol ester' the unique cholesterol lowering ingredient.

It does this by partly blocking the entry of cholesterol into the bloodstream.

Plant stanol is a substance that occurs naturally in small amounts in many grains, vegetables, fruits, legumes, nuts and seeds.

There are over 80 clinical studies which prove that plant stanols are among the few nutritional components that can truly lower cholesterol.

They also state: A daily intake of 1.5–2.4 g plant stanols lowers cholesterol by 7–10% in 2 to 3 weeks.

It was recommended to me by my doctor, as part of a life-style change, and I've been taking it now as a yoghurt drink, daily, for many years.

I believe it is a factor in reducing my cholesterol levels.

Each small bottle – 67.5 g contains 2g of plant stanols which help lower cholesterol.

The packaging also states: "Heart disease can have multiple factors and you may need to change more than one to lower overall risk."

So take an holistic approach – look at all aspects of your life.

Naturally, it's difficult to know how much difference it has made, but my view is that based on doctor's advice, and linked with other changes, it's better to take it than not.

Views and Observations

"...We no longer sit around a table to eat... there's no knife and fork eating, it's mostly finger food now... grazing seems to be what most people do – the idea of three meals a day is history now... I think it's better to have some sort of structure to your eating... otherwise you just graze all day on rubbish food!"
Richard, 61, managed BP and Chol

"...I read in some Gov nanny literature about diet, to eat lobster no more than twice a week and avoid offal... and remove the salt pot from the table... I thought which century are they living in, and WTAF is offal?? So no more medieval banquets for us then... Advice like this is nonsense and isn't relatable for us normal people... I like your constructive and straightforward advice to check food labels for fat and salt content and look for 'exchange' foods when moving to a healthier diet..."
Ed, 56, managed BP and Chol

"...I realised that two or three takeaways per week wasn't healthy so I've reduced it to one per week... eventually it will be one per month..."
David, 55, managed BP and Chol

"...My Hebridean Granny used to say 'eat well is shit well's brother'... I reckon she had a point there..."
Janice, 45, fit and healthy

TIP
Make changes to your diet gradually and have an 'exchange' food in place before giving something up completely.

REFLECTION
"Eat half, walk double, laugh triple, love without measure." *Tibetan proverb*

Where are you now?

Body shape and weight.

As a starting point, where do you think you are now:

- Slim Jim
- Average
- Couch potato
- Porky
- Two ton Tess
- Fat f*cker

Where would you like to be?

Plan of Action

Jot down here, or on a separate piece of paper, or in the 'Notes' section of your phone or tablet, what action you intend to take.

Monitor weight

Guidance on BMI – *see nhs.uk*

5

...Exercise is also essential for immune system functionality – this helps you to fight disease and infection...

Step 5
Exercise

The word exercise or gym strikes fear into most normal people. Who wants to waste time sweating in a gym with other sweaty people, most of whom are going to be fitter than you anyway.

It's important because it strengthens your heart and keeps you healthier, and increases the volume of your arteries.

You grow blood vessels when you exercise consistently – use them or lose them.

It's a little known fact that the word 'exercise' is derived from the Latin *exercisorum* which means 'profit for sports shops'.

Athleisure is a terrible portmanteau word – two words joined together – that sums it up. All the gear, no idea.

You could go out and buy the 'athleisure' kit in preparation for a new exercise regime. Or just wear the clothes without actually doing the exercising.

Get your excuses in first, obvs.

Here are a few:

- Too busy
- Nike VapourFly running shoes not yet arrived
- Mate, work has been manic

- The dog ate my shorts
- Flu
- Man flu
- Too tired
- Looks like rain
- Those box sets won't watch themselves
- Nando's had a special offer

When considering exercise, you mutter a phrase which involves the words: "...that for a game of soldiers..." and go back to sitting and staring at a screen. Most of us are very good at that and if it were an olympic sport we'd all be gold medallists. You know how it is: feet up on the sofa, watching TV, phone in hand and tablet on your lap while you manage all three effortlessly, and of course polishing off a tube of Pringles.

But of course on the podium we'd be scrolling through our phones checking for 'likes' on Insta and so on.

The experts trot out the mantra: 'eat less, move more' but it's just blah, blah, blah and whatever.

The ideal is to find ways that suit you, and work for you rather than a 'one size fits all' lazy stereotype shoved at us by the government health nannies.

Find something you enjoy doing and just move – it could be walking, dancing, swimming, Zumba, Ceroc, cycling, press ups, star jumps, horizontal jogging [with another person], yoga, pilates and so on.

Exercise to the point of being slightly breathless. The Borg Scale [*see Glossary*] measures exertion on a scale of 6–20.

Even housework could get you moving – think Freddie Mercury hoovering on [earworm warning] 'I want to break free.' Or washing the car by hand, gardening, playing with your children or grand children or even walking to the shops.

Little and often is usually better and more accessible.

For exercising indoors you could watch exercise videos on YouTube.

Here's an idea: use the lowest step to step up and down six times before going upstairs.

The important thing is to move your body to exercise it and move away from a sedentary lifestyle where we sit at desks and stare at a screen. And yes, I am sitting at a desk and staring at a screen as I write this.

Naturally, I will offset that very shortly by starting a gruelling two-hour gym session of bench pressing, glutes, reps, triceps, chest and core exercises. Nah! Not really, but I will do something that works for me – a 10 minute row while I watch something on the iPad. That's on the rowing machine, btw, not a shouting match with the wife.

What also worked for me was regularly walking with a purpose. I don't like walking just for the sake of it so we started planning walks with points of interest en route. This made the walk secondary to exploring new places of interest.

This led to *[shameless book plug]* writing the book *12 Bridges. London* which uses 12 of the capital's bridges as starting points with interesting things to look at or search for, on walks lasting around one hour.

Views and Observations

"...I got over the inertia by just taking a walk in my work clothes... I realised that I'd been making excuses not to exercise... such as not having the right kit with me..."
Steve, 55, managed BP and Chol

"...What worked for me was having weights and resistance bands in the sitting room so rather than have a separate 'exercise' room I'd just work out wherever I was... so when I got a spare 10 mins I'd use the weights or bands..."
Chris, 59, managed BP and Chol

"...I put on my favourite song and dance to that, I know its only 3m 34s so it's a high intensity work out for me!"
Sue, 53, managed BP and Chol

"...That six steps on the lowest stair worked for me as a starting point... I then challenged myself to do more and more... baby steps and all that!"
Donna, 55, managed BP and Chol

"...I've been getting off the bus a stop earlier and walking... I know it's not much but it's a start..."
Nigel, 60, managed BP and Chol

"...Walking once a day for around 40/45 minutes has made a considerable difference... my BP has gone down by 10%... I'm happy with that and now I'm sucking diesel!"
Patrick, 58, managed BP

So if you only do one thing, start with six steps of exercise. Stepping up and back down six times on the lowest step of a staircase.

Do try this at home. Not on the London Tube system though. Although we're a generally friendly bunch in London, you'd be likely to hear shouts of: "Get out of the *%@*@ing way!"

Which would stress you. And increase your blood pressure.

Keep in mind that some exercise needs to be aerobic – where you get out of breath – as increasing your metabolic rate burns LDL [Lower Density Lipoproteins – the 'bad' cholesterol] and other blood fats.

Exercise is also essential for immune system functionality – this helps you to fight disease and infection.

Drinking alcohol, smoking and poor nutrition are not good for your immune system.

TIP

Don't make all the changes at once. Find ways of exercising which suit you and fit into your lifestyle and time, rather than conform to pressure from others or social media.

If you haven't exercised for years, start gradually and build up slowly.

6

...Where possible, look for areas in your life where you can reduce stress. Sometimes it's the small things that can have the biggest effect...

Step 6
Lifestyle

Take a more relaxed view and avoid situations which might stress you and cause your blood pressure to rise.

This could be when driving, queuing at the shops, if an argument arises with colleagues, friends and family, meeting deadlines, rushing to get things done and so on.

Stress

Where possible – look for areas in your life where you can reduce stress. Sometimes it's the small things that can have the biggest effect.

Imagine if the stress of having an argument over a car parking space at Morrisons resulted in you having a heart attack over something as trivial as to who got to a parking bay first. It's not worth it.

Imagine the conversations as you lay dying on the floor by your car… onlookers gather round, phones out, filming you. One says: "Anybody phoned for an ambulance?" Someone else says: "Yeah, I think that guy over there did."

"Oh, OK. Have you seen this funny cat video, it looks like Hitler, sort of furred reich!?"

Your life is in YOUR hands. Don't let some random person be the cause of your death.

Mind you, at Waitrose it would be a quite different story. Posh woman standing by a massive, wonkily parked 4×4 says: "Oh, poor you. Wait there and I'll get someone to see to you. Let me take a pic so the staff know what you look like. First though I need to stock up on quinoa and kale as we're having a supper party tonight."

Seriously though, is it worth getting wound up over trivial matters? Would you want your last vision to be of strangers peering down at you, filming you and then showing their mates in the pub later, saying: "Have a look at this – some old geezer croaked it in the car park. To be fair, he didn't look well. Now, whose round is it?"

You end up as a clip on random strangers' phones. Just a few seconds of 'entertainment' in a day's worth of gifs, memes and WhatsApp. Then you're instantly forgotten.

Views and Observations

"...It was stress at work that caused my high blood pressure... I was drinking as well to cope with the stress and that made it even worse... I was short-tempered and taking it out on my family... I felt like a pressure cooker ready to explode... I stopped drinking and took more exercise... the BP tablets helped as well and now my BP is back to normal... and most importantly, my family now have me back as the dad they knew before..."
Dave, 52, managed BP

"...I'd always be up for an argument, or wind people up just for a laugh... once I discovered I had high blood pressure I decided to take a more chilled approach... it's worked and I find different ways of dealing with people, looking for another way rather than just going at it like a bull in a china shop... I surprised myself with

the outcomes which were often better than before... it's a win-win, I maintain my blood pressure at a reasonable level and other people think I'm a good guy, taking a reasonable view and being prepared to compromise..."
Laurence, 50, managed BP and Chol

"...I used to be one of those drivers who always had to be in front at the lights... or when two lanes merged into one I'd always make the other driver's decision for him and edge him out... sometimes there'd be a bit of effing and jeffing and I enjoyed that... I realised that it probably did raise my blood pressure so now I'm much more amenable and let people in... I'm constantly amazed at how grateful people are and the feeling it gives me when you get the thumbs up, smile, the four-way flashers... I think the Americans call it the 'warm fuzzies' and I'm truly surprised how it made me feel... mind you, I often draw level, or ahead of them at the next set of lights or roundabout hehehe..."
Barry, 54, managed BP and Chol

"...One of the blokes at work had died from a heart attack... just keeled over dropped down dead... always seemed fit and never had any time off... I think he did a bit of running as well... such a shame... he was only 57... had a family as well..."
Terry, 56, and now regularly checking BP and Cholesterol

More males than females suffer heart attacks and stroke. This is because we take more risks and have more highly stressed, rufty-tufty jobs and lifestyles – oh yeah, such as web designers, content providers, writers, call centre staff and so on.

Naturally, the little ladies lead a stress-free life just shopping and baking, gossiping about make-up and such like, being home-makers.*

*This is, obviously, very sarcastic and highly inappropriate and doesn't recognise that women lead full and busy lives these days and are of course equal to and in some cases superior to menfolk [or so the wife says...]**

**When I was dictating the above I had my fingers crossed behind my back so it doesn't count.

The real reason that males suffer more heart attacks – twice as many as women – is due to the fact that the genetic disposition to heart disease is passed on through the male line.

So to quote the famous poem by Philip Larkin: "They f*ck you up, your mum and dad... and fill you with all the faults they had... And add some extra just for you..." It seems that your dad though will f*ck you up even worse. Gee, thanks for nothing, dad.

There is some evidence that a person's ethnic background could make them more pre-disposed to heart attacks than others. Likely causes include a high fat diet [for example using ghee to cook with], rich food, cultural attitudes to eating, and genetics.

Please Note: there is a specific genetic [male] heart condition which causes some incidences of, often fatal, heart attacks, usually in very fit men who aren't necessarily 'blowing their top' all the time.

On the other hand the instances caused by the sort of stress being described earlier may be different and due to a build-up of poorly managed stress events – and even big events in someone's life.

As well as looking for ways to reduce stress – it cannot be reduced completely – try also:

Relaxation Techniques

- Breathing out for twice as long as breathing in
- Counting to 10
- Practising Mindfulness: Take time out of your day to pause and be a Human 'Being' – rather than a Human 'Doing'
- Spending some time doing enjoyable and relaxing things, for example, reading/music
- Improving time management such as allowing more time for a journey

TIP

Make changes to your lifestyle to reduce the risk of stroke or heart attack.

Sufficient good quality sleep is also an important part of lifestyle to help reduce blood pressure.

If you always do what you've always done you'll always get what you always got. If nothing changes, nothing will change.

REFLECTION

You don't have to see the whole staircase – just look at the first six steps.

...The key is to drink in moderation, allowing clear days so that your body – particularly the liver – can recover...

Alcohol

How does alcohol affect blood pressure and cholesterol?

Drinking too much alcohol can raise the levels of some fats in the blood known as triglycerides.

A high blood fat triglyceride level combined with high LDL (bad) cholesterol or low HDL (good) cholesterol has been associated with fatty build up in the artery walls, which narrows them. This means that the heart has to work harder to pump blood through narrower tubes.

That, in turn, can increase the risk of heart attack and stroke.

How much is too much and should you drink at all?

Do not drink regularly per week more than 14 units of alcohol: 6 pints of beer [4% abv], or 6 × 175ml glasses of wine [13%abv] or 14 × 25ml glasses of whisky [40%abv]. *Source: Chief Medical Officer's .gov guidelines.*

These guidelines are now the same for men and women. They also reduce the risks of cancer and other diseases.

However, if you're pregnant you shouldn't drink alcohol at all.

Ideally, no more than 2 drinks [glasses/pints] per day, with 2 sober days in between is also a safe guideline.

Binge-drinking will significantly increase your chances of raised blood pressure.

The key is to drink in moderation, allowing clear

days so that your body – particularly the liver – can recover.

The increase in blood pressure is irrespective of the type of alcohol consumed.

Alcohol also contains a lot of calories and sugar which can cause weight gain which in turn can increase your blood pressure.

It also increases the desire for food when and after you drink – kebab on the way home?

> **TIP**
> Reduce your alcohol intake to reduce your blood pressure and cholesterol.

Where are you now?

Alcoholic Units per week.

- ☐ Zero
- ☐ 1–5 units per week
- ☐ 6–10 units per week
- ☐ 10+ units per week
- ☐ 20+ units per week
- ☐ Paralytic – losshtt count!

Where would you like to be?

Plan of Action

Jot down here, or on a separate piece of paper, or in the 'Notes' section of your phone or tablet, what action you intend to take.

Smoking

How does smoking affect blood pressure and cholesterol?

How much, and should you smoke or vape at all?

Smoking can increase your blood pressure because the nicotine in smoke can harden and narrow your arteries making it more difficult for the blood to be pumped around your body.

The chemicals in tobacco can also damage the lining of your artery walls. And can damage the lungs with tar deposits.

Your blood is more likely to clot, and chances increase of a heart attack, stroke or lung damage.

Vaping is lower risk but will still cause an increase in heart rate and blood pressure.

TIP
Reduce your smoking or quit altogether, to reduce your blood pressure and cholesterol.

Where are you now?

Cigarettes per week:

☐ Zero
☐ 1–5 per week
☐ 6–10 per week
☐ 10+ per week
☐ 20+ per day
☐ Fag ash Lil

Where would you like to be?

Plan of Action

Jot down on a piece of paper, or in the 'Notes' section of your phone or tablet, what action you intend to take.

...Why should you not take the tablets with grapefruit or grapefruit juice?

FAQs

Frequently asked questions – with answers – about blood pressure and cholesterol.

1. At what age should blood pressure start to be monitored?
Generally at 40-years-old, when our bodies start to decline naturally. However, no reason why you shouldn't start at an earlier age and be aware of what your BP is, and monitor it from then on perhaps annually, changing to monthly at age 40, weekly at 50 and daily from 60 onwards.

2. Does it matter which arm you use to take blood pressure on?
No. Be consistent though and use the same arm each time. It's a myth that the left arm should be used as it's closer to the heart. For right-handed people it's usually easier to attach the cuff to the left arm.

3. When should you take BP and Cholesterol tablets – statins?
They can be taken morning or evening, there's no real difference. If you feel fatigued, it may be better to take the statins [a possible cause] in the evening, just before you go to bed.

4. Can you take them together?
Yes – you can then be sure of taking both of them.

A pill box with compartments for each day of the week can help you to remember to take them each day. Tip: leave the lid open once you've taken the tablet as an extra reminder. And of course, Wednesday, Thursday and Friday will spell out WTF [not big, not clever but still quite amusing].

5. Why should you not take the tablets with grapefruit or grapefruit juice?
An active ingredient in grapefruit prohibits the drugs working effectively. Leave at least 4 hours before drinking grapefruit juice or eating grapefruit and taking the tablets or better still – avoid grapefruit altogether.

6. What happens if I miss a day's tablets?
Don't take double the amount but just take the usual prescribed amount the next day.

7. If I go on holiday and forget my tablets what should I do?
Visit a pharmacy and ask for their advice. Make sure you take a note of your prescribed tablets and dosage. A photo of the box would also help.

8. What time of day should I take my blood pressure?
Ideally in the morning before your day starts. This ensures the figures are taken whilst you're still and calm. If you took it at midday the readings would be higher and skewed by activity, events or stress during the morning.

9. How many readings should I take?
Take three and either take an average of them, or the lowest one. Consider that the first one may be slightly higher if you're not fully relaxed and calm.

10. Should I worry if I get one reading that is high?
An isolated blip could have many causes – stress at work, an event that worries you and so on.

Monitor your readings and if you get three high readings over three days then contact your GP.

It's patterns of high readings that you should be aware of rather than random spikes which are quite usual.

11. How should I record my blood pressure?
Use a notebook and write the numbers in each day, enter them in a diary or journal

or set up a template in the 'Notes' section on your phone or tablet.

12. Is it true that you smell toast when a heart attack or stroke is imminent?

It's a myth. There's no evidence that this is the case. The sense of smell can be enhanced but there's no particular smell you should worry about.

13. Why do heart attacks happen on the loo and sometimes in the middle of the night?

Discomfort in the stomach – a possible sign of an imminent heart attack – can lead you to feel that you need a poo. This leads you to get out of bed and sit on the loo. Also straining to poo will put extra pressure on the heart.

Other signs of an impending heart attack are an uncomfortable pressure, squeezing or pain in the upper body areas including arms, the back, the neck or jaw.

Also feeling sick and light-headed.

Note: Elvis Presley died on the loo in the middle of the night with a cheeseburger in his hand.

Don't be like Elvis – his last great hit was the bathroom floor!

14. What should I do if I suspect I'm having a heart attack or stroke?

Call 999 immediately and rest while you wait for an ambulance to avoid unnecessary strain on your heart.

Rather than lie down, half-sit up – for example sitting on the floor with your back resting against a sofa – with your knees bent.

If aspirin is available, and you're not allergic to it, slowly chew and then swallow a tablet while you wait for an ambulance.

Aspirin helps to thin the blood and improve flow to the heart.

15. And if I suspect someone else is having a heart attack or stroke?

Call 999 immediately and advise the patient to rest while you wait for an ambulance to avoid unnecessary strain on the heart.

Rather than lie down, half-sit up – for example sitting on the floor with their back resting against a sofa – with knees bent.

If aspirin is available, and they're not allergic to it, get them to chew slowly and then swallow a tablet while they wait for an ambulance.

Aspirin helps to thin the blood and improve flow to the heart.

16. Should CPR [Cardio Pulmonary Rescue] be used on heart attack victims?

Only if they go into cardiac arrest, become unconscious and are not breathing.

CPR will keep the heart going while waiting for an ambulance. Push down hard and fast in the centre of the chest at a rate of 100–120 pushes per minute. Do this to the rhythm of [appropriately] 'Staying alive' by the Bee Gees.

Keep going until the person shows signs of recovery: opening eyes, coughing, breathing or speaking. Or until the paramedics arrive to take over.

Q&A With The Author

Brian M Stratton

Q1. How did you discover you had high blood pressure?
"A routine visit to the doctor on an unrelated matter. That was in 2017 and the reading was 168/98, much higher than the standard maximum of 140/90. Since then it has been managed and monitored on a regular basis. Naturally, I was concerned that it was so high, but I was even more concerned that I'd got to the age of 60 and didn't know about high blood pressure or cholesterol. It had never been on my radar. Why not?"

Q2. How fit would you say you are now – on a scale of 1–10?
"Reasonably good. I feel fit and everything is in good working order – touch wood – on a scale of 1–10 I'd say a solid 8."

Q3. What's your height, weight and generalhealth?
"Height is 1.88m [6'1"] and weight is 82kg [12st 9lb] and a healthy BMI number of 23. General health is good – still have all my own teeth – and like most people of my age [vintage 1956] sometimes have the odd ache or twinge. But definitely many more good days than not. My blood pressure is controlled and averages out at 136/86 and cholesterol averages at 4."

Q4. What's your exercise routine now?
"A couple of visits to the gym during the week, some free weights and rowing at home and most weekends a walk of 5–7 miles."

Q5. How did you decide on an exercise routine that suits you?
"I realised that rather than competing against others, I would just focus on myself. Yeah, I know, it's me, me, me!

There will always be someone fitter, stronger and more ripped than you so it's pointless to try and compete.

Work out where you're at now, where you want to be and how to get there.

Social media can present a distorted view of others' 'perfect' lives and we can tend to judge our lives on the trailer of others compared to the full length movie version of our own. It's just they might be better at taking pics, editing and curating them to show themselves in the best light.

Be true to yourself and be the best version of yourself that you can be. I also look at the time spent on exercising as 30 minutes watching a programme on the iPad while I'm doing something else [exercising] so the main event for me is catching up on programmes, not the 'boring' stuff."

Q6. What were the two life-changing potentially fatal events you referred to in the introduction?

"The first was a head-on collision with a drunk driver more than twenty years' ago.

The result was several broken bones and a hospital stay of a month, followed by months of physio. Then I got back on with life.

The next – which was five years' ago – was contracting Legionnaires Disease or as the Daily Mail call it: 'Deadly Killer Disease!' And had I been 10 years older and not so fit it would have been fatal. The result was being rushed into hospital and a hospital stay of a week, followed by convalescing. Then I got back on with life.

Coincidentally, with both of the above I was in the same hospital, in the same ward, albeit 15 years apart. What hadn't changed was hospital visitors complaining about the car park charges.

Once I'd fully recovered from the Legionnaires Disease I was chatting to my doctor about it.

In 35 years' of general practice he'd never had a case of this before. After all, it's not something you'd expect in suburban London.

Mind you, I think he was secretly pleased as he'd probably had it on his bucket list and had now ticked it off. I reckon the only one he hadn't encountered was Bubonic Plague.

Just out of interest, I asked what would have happened if I hadn't been rushed into hospital on the Friday night. He said, in a matter-of-fact manner: "You probably wouldn't have survived until the Monday morning."

So in 48 hours that would have been that.

At this point the hairs on the back of my neck stood on end, and a chill ran through my body.

*I thought: 'F**k!!! That was close!!!'*

I said, trying to keep things normal: "So, any holidays planned yet, doctor?"

There's also a third event: when I was six I got run over when I was chasing a girl across a road. Did it hurt? You bet – to this day she's never written, or phoned... And there was the time when, aged three and very inquisitive, I stuck my finger into an electric socket and got a burnt fingernail.

I had all the usual childhood ailments that were doing the rounds in the 50s and 60s: diphtheria, whooping cough, scarlet fever, mumps, measles, chicken pox and so on [childhood diseases bingo – full house]. It was a case of take the medicine and get on with it.

I wonder how today's snowflakes would cope with all of that...

There were also visits to A&E for various childhood scrapes involving crashing bikes, stone-throwing incidents and other general mishaps.

Other minor abrasions were usually fixed by a spit on a hankie which was then rubbed on to the affected area, or in extreme cases a dose of TCP or Germolene and a plaster. Job done. Get on with it.

If it was something really serious you'd be confined to bed and left with a bottle of Lucozade in a pimply glass bottle wrapped in crinkly orange cellophane on your bedside table."

Q7. How have you changed what you eat?

"I never thought I'd say this but I feel much healthier since changing what I eat and considering more carefully the content of food in terms of salt, fat and so on.

The difference is that I feel lighter and less sluggish than before. You know the energy drop you get after lunch around 2pm, well I rarely have those now and feel more energised.

I think what made the most difference was discovering the Traffic Light system on food packaging.

What a great idea – why didn't someone think about that before? My wife has just said it's been in for about 20 years. It's just I'd never bothered to look before.

My visits to a supermarket were a quick runaround, chuck things in a trolley, pay and get out as quickly as possible.

Mind you, in Aldi there was always the central aisle 'Special Buys' or, [very] random stuff – inflatable canoe, axe or 72-piece tool-kit that occasionally distracted me.

Previously I'd thought it was just weirdos that stood and peered at labels.

But they could save your life! Who knew?

Just a slight whinge though – why do they have to print them so small? Us Oldies who need to read them also need reading glasses or if we've forgotten them hold the packet at arm's length to read what is written in a microscopic font like this.

But such a good idea and very helpful when deciding what to buy [OK Boomer, as the kids would surely say today].

See it as a 'red light means danger' sign.

If you buy that foodstuff with a red marking is it going to increase or decrease your risk of dying earlier?

It's a no-brainer."

Notes

Jot down here, or on a separate piece of paper, or in the 'Notes' section of your phone or tablet, what action you intend to take.

...Blood Pressure – The force at which blood is pumped around your heart. Too high or too low is unhealthy...

Glossary

Explanation of Terms

Angina Chest pain caused by reduced blood flow to the heart muscles. It can be an early sign that you're at risk of a heart attack.

Blood Pressure The force at which blood is pumped around your heart. Too high or too low is unhealthy.

BMI Body Mass Index. This uses your height and weight to arrive at a BMI figure, which is measured against a chart to give an indicator of the correct height/weight ratio and health status. For adults, the ideal range is 18.5 – 24.9

Borg Scale The Borg Rating of Perceived Exertion (RPE) scale, developed by Swedish researcher Gunnar Borg, is a tool for measuring an individual's effort and exertion, breathlessness and fatigue during physical work.

Cholesterol A waxy substance found in blood. Too much can cause fatty deposits and this can lead to higher blood pressure.

Clogged Arteries The build up of fatty or fibrous material inside the arteries, causing them to be narrowed and restricting the supply of blood to the heart or brain.

Diabetes A condition whereby your pancreas can't make enough insulin and you end up with high blood sugar levels.

There are two different types:

Type 1 – as above.

Type 2 – where the liver and muscles are resistant to taking up sugar, leaving high levels in the bloodstream, this is often caused by being overweight.

Diastolic The lower number of a blood pressure reading. For example: 140/90. 90 is the diastolic number or the pressure when the heart is resting between beats.

FAST A way to remember the signs and symptoms of a TIA or Stroke:

F ace – the face may have dropped on one side and person may not be able to smile, or their mouth or eye may have drooped

A rms – the person may not be able to lift both arms and keep them there: could be weakness or numbness in one arm

S peech – may be slurred or garbled, or the person may not be able to talk. They may not understand what you say to them

T ime – time to act fast and dial 999 for an ambulance if you notice these signs

Fatty Liver This happens when too much fat builds up in the liver. Can be caused by high cholesterol, obesity, alcohol, energy drinks plus poor diet and lack of exercise.

HDL High Density Lipids – known as 'good' cholesterol which helps to balance out the LDL 'bad' cholesterol.

Heart Attack A medical emergency when the blood supply to the heart is suddenly blocked, often by a blood clot. *See also FAST*

LDL Low Density Lipids – known as 'bad' cholesterol because it can form plaque which adheres to the artery walls, ultimately narrowing them, clogging them and possibly leading to a heart attack or stroke.

Statins Drugs prescribed to lower cholesterol levels in the blood. Avoid drinking grapefruit juice or grapefruit itself when taking statins. The reason is that the drug's effect is reduced. Allow a four hour window before or after eating grapefruit or drinking the juice.

Stroke This happens when the blood supply to part of the brain is cut off by a clot. It can occur when blood pressure reaches 180/120 or higher. At this level there is an 80% chance of stroke within 12 months.

It's called a stroke because it looks as if you have been 'stroked' down one side: causing the face to droop on one side. *See also FAST*

Superfoods Healthy foods said to bestow positive health effects. The list could include: kale, blueberries, green tea, nuts and seeds, turmeric amongst others.

Systolic The top number of a blood pressure reading, for example: 140/90. 140 is the systolic number, measuring the pressure when the heart is pumping out the blood around the body.

TIA Transient Ischaemic Attack: a mini stroke. It's a warning that you're at risk of having a full stroke in the near future. *See also FAST*

White Coat Syndrome When you visit the doctor and your blood pressure is increased. It is so-called because doctors used to wear white coats, causing us to be anxious, linked to being in a surgery or hospital setting.

6 Steps Summary: Fix in Six

iOS: In One Sentence

Step 1: Measure
Measure your blood pressure and cholesterol and note it down in the space at end of this summary

Step 2: Manage
If your BP and cholesterol is high, manage it with advice from your GP and medication if required

Step 3: Monitor
Monitor your numbers on a regular basis to ensure consistency and to be aware early of any changes

Step 4: Diet
Consider changes to your diet to ensure BP and cholesterol levels are reduced where necessary and then maintained at a healthy level

Step 5: Exercise
Take regular exercise – in a form that suits you and that you find enjoyable

Step 6: Lifestyle
Assess your lifestyle and consider the stressful elements, and develop coping strategies to reduce the stress

To Do List

The First 6 Steps | 6 for Success

Buy Blood Pressure monitor

Done: ______

Date: ______

Buy self-test cholesterol kit

Done: ______

Date: ______

Change one item of food to healthier options

Done: ______

Date: ______

Reduce alcohol intake by one drink per week

Done: ______

Date: ______

Cut down smoking by two cigarettes per day

Done: ______

Date: ______

Use the first step of the stairs to do 6 steps

Done: ______

Date: ______

And Finally...

All of the time you've been reading this book your heart has been working for you. Silent, uncomplaining and just doing what it should.

So why don't you do some work for your heart to repay it for keeping you alive and healthy all of these years.

Make it smile.

Look after it, and it will look after you.

So do something.

Not tomorrow.

Not next week.

Now.

Over to you...

Further Information

You may find the following websites useful for further research and information:

nhs.uk

bhf.org

bloodpressureuk.org

heart.org.uk

drinkaware.co.uk

medicalnewstoday.com

niddk.nih.gov

***Disclaimer:** please note that I'm not medically trained so any changes to your health routine should in the first instance be discussed with your GP and/or other health professionals.*